A Gift For

FROM:

....

Are You Talking

Guidelines
for Life from

Eugene H. Peterson

to Me, God?

J. Countryman NASHVILLE, TENNESSEE

CONTENTS

Talking About...

Wise Choices

God is the center from which all life develops.

Teach me
how to live to please you,
because you're my God.

PSALM 143:8

Get wisdom—
it's worth more than money;
choose insight over income
every time.

PROVERBS 16:16

Wise men and women
are always learning,
always listening for fresh insights.

PROVERBS 18:15

Everyone
has choices to make.
The choices are
not trial-and-error guesses;
they are informed by the
commands of God.

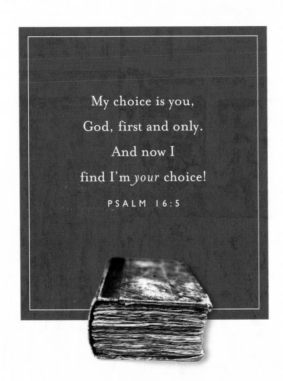

My choice is you,
God, first and only.
And now I
find I'm *your* choice!

PSALM 16:5

- Work your garden—
  you'll end up with plenty of food;
  play and party—
  you'll end up with an empty plate.

PROVERBS 28:20

- It's better to be wise than strong;
  intelligence outranks muscle any day.

PROVERBS 24:5

- Keep the rules and keep your life;
  careless living kills.

PROVERBS 19:16

Our lives are not
puzzles to be figured out.
Rather, we come to God,
who knows us and reveals to us
the truth of our lives.
The fundamental mistake is
to begin with ourselves
and not God.

Knowing what is right is like
deep water in the heart; a wise person
draws from the well within.

———————

Show me how you work,
God; school me in your ways.

PSALM 25:4

Talking About...

Plans for Success

If we live in hope we go against the stream.

There is an
enormous gap between
what we think we can do
and what God calls us to do.
Our ideas of what we can
do or want to do are trivial;
God's ideas for us
are grand.

- Refuse good advice and watch
  your plans fail;
  take good counsel
  and watch them succeed.

  PROVERBS 15:22

- Don't jump to conclusions—
  there may be a perfectly good explanation
  for what you just saw.

  PROVERBS 25:8

- Generous hands are blessed hands
  because they give bread to the poor.

  PROVERBS 22:9

- GOD cares about honesty in the workplace;
  your business is his business.

  PROVERBS 16:11

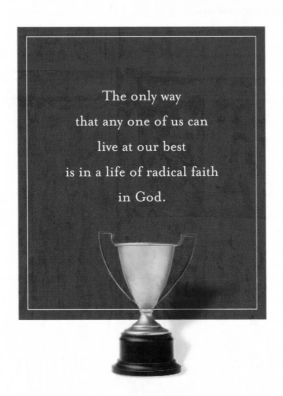

The only way
that any one of us can
live at our best
is in a life of radical faith
in God.

You're blessed
when you stay on course,
walking steadily on the road revealed by God.
You're blessed
when you follow his directions,
doing your best to find him.

PSALM 119:1–2

———

Careful planning
puts you ahead in the long run;
hurry and scurry puts you
further behind.

PROVERBS 21:5

———

You need to stick it out,
staying with God's plan so you'll
be there for the promised completion.

HEBREWS 10:36

Talking About...

Tuned to
Truth

Our beliefs shape our behavior.

However exalted
the truths of God, they are
not too great or too high
to be experienced
by ordinary people in the
minutiae of the everyday.

Your words all add up to
the sum total: Truth.

PSALM 119:160

———————

Your words are so choice,
so tasty;
I prefer them to the
best home cooking.

PSALM 119:103

- God is doing what is best for us,
  training us to live God's holy best.

HEBREWS 12:10

- God wants us to grow up,
  to know the whole truth and tell it
  in love—like Christ in everything.

EPHESIANS 4:15

- GOD, teach me lessons for living
  so I can stay the course.

PSALM 119:33

Christian discipleship is a
decision to walk in God's ways,
steadily and firmly....
It is the way of life we were
created for.

We must learn
to live by the truth,
not by our feelings,
not by the world's opinion,
... not by what
advertisers tell us is the most
gratifying lifestyle.

- What you say goes, God, and *stays,*
  as permanent as the heavens.
  Your truth never goes out of fashion.

PSALM 119:89–90

- Oh! Teach us to live well!
  Teach us to live wisely and well!

PSALM 90:12

- Your righteousness is eternally right,
  your revelation is the only truth.

PSALM 119:142

- Give yourself to disciplined instruction;
  open your ears to tested knowledge.

PROVERBS 23:11

Talking About...

People

(forget Perfect)

Every act of love is a risk of the self.

The command
we have from Christ is blunt:
Loving God
includes loving people.

1 JOHN 4:21

- Mostly what God does is love you. Keep
  company with him and learn a life of love.

  EPHESIANS 5:1

- Don't compare yourself with others.
  Each of you must take responsibility for
  doing the creative best you can
  with your own life.

  GALATIANS 6:5

- Love other people as well as you do yourself.
  You can't go wrong when you love others.

  ROMANS 13:9

- Welcome with open arms fellow believers
  who don't see things the way you do. . . .
  Eventually, we're all going to end up
  kneeling side by side . . . facing God.

  ROMANS 14:1, 10

Love . . .
puts up with anything, trusts God always,
always looks for the best.

I CORINTHIANS 13:7

We will not compare
ourselves with each other as if
one of us were better and another worse.
We have far more interesting things
to do with our lives.

GALATIANS 5:26

Regarding life together
and getting along with each other . . .
just love one another!

I THESSALONIANS 4:9

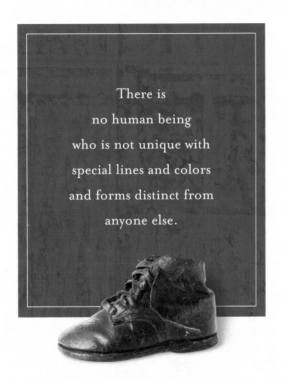

There is
no human being
who is not unique with
special lines and colors
and forms distinct from
anyone else.

Talking About...

Solving Problems

Freedom comes from trusting,...
from leaving matters to God.

Don't fret or worry.
Instead of worrying, pray.
Let petitions
and praises shape your
worries into prayers,
letting God know your
concerns.

PHILIPPIANS 4:6

One righteous
will outclass fifty wicked,
for the wicked are moral weaklings but
the righteous are God-strong.

PSALM 37:16–17

Steep your life in God-reality,
God-initiative, God-provisions. . . .
You'll find all your everyday human
concerns will be met.

MATTHEW 6:33

- We can be sure that every detail
  in our lives of love for God is worked
  into something good.

  ROMANS 8:28

- You call out to God for help
  and he helps.

  I PETER 1:17

- Absolutely *nothing* can get
  between us and God's love.

  ROMANS 8:39

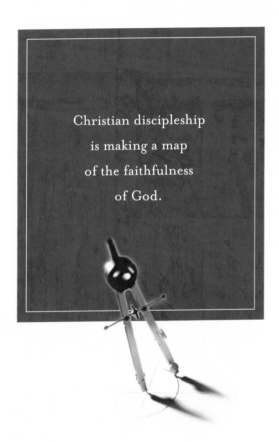

Christian discipleship
is making a map
of the faithfulness
of God.

i know what i'm doing.
i have it all planned out—
plans to take care of you,
not abandon you,
plans to give you
the future you hope for.

JEREMIAH 29:11

Hoping is

not dreaming....

It means a confident,

alert expectation that God will

do what he said he will do.

Talking About...
A Passion for
Purity

The art of saying no sets us free to follow Jesus.

Following Jesus
means not following your
impulses and appetites
and whims and dreams,
all of which are
sufficiently damaged by sin
to make them
unreliable guides for getting
anyplace worth going.

- Live in such a way
  that you are a credit
  to the Message of Christ.

  PHILIPPIANS 1:27

- Since the Master honors you with a body,
  honor him with your body!

  I CORINTHIANS 6:13

- Run for dear life from evil;
  hold on for dear life to good.

  ROMANS 12:9

- Run away from infantile indulgence.
  Run after mature righteousness.

  2 TIMOTHY 2:22

You're addicted to thrills?

What an empty life!

The pursuit of pleasure is

never satisfied.

PROVERBS 21:17

Anyone
and everyone is able
to live a zestful life
that spills out of the
stereotyped containers
a sin-inhibited society
provides.

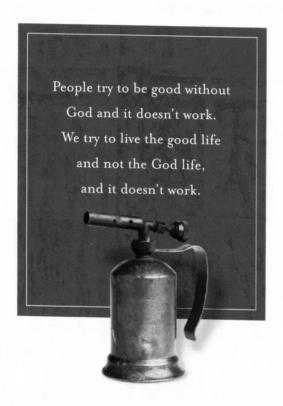

People try to be good without
God and it doesn't work.
We try to live the good life
and not the God life,
and it doesn't work.

- Think straight.
  Awaken to the holiness of life....
  Ignorance of God is a luxury you can't
  afford in times like these.

  1 CORINTHIANS 15:34

- Let's make our entire lives fit and holy
  temples for the worship of God.

  2 CORINTHIANS 7:1

- Let every detail in your lives—
  words, actions, whatever—
  be done in the name of
  the Master, Jesus.

  COLOSSIANS 3:17

Talking About...

Uniquely You

*The Christian life
is a dancing,
leaping, daring life.*

With God
I am not a zero.
Not a minus.
I have a set-apart place
that only I can fill.

Are You Talking to Me God?

- You shaped me first inside,
  then out; you formed me
  in my mother's womb.

  PSALM 139:13

- With your very own hands
  you formed me; now breathe
  your wisdom over me.

  PSALM 119:73

- You know exactly how I was made,
  bit by bit, how I was sculpted from
  nothing into something.

  PSALM 139:15

- Embracing what God does for you
  is the best thing you can do for him.

  ROMANS 12:1

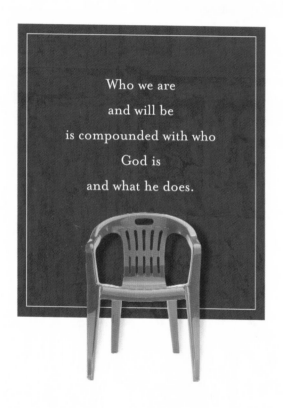

Who we are
and will be
is compounded with who
God is
and what he does.

Not one of us,
at this moment,
is complete.
In another hour,
another day,
we will have changed.
We are in process of becoming
either less or more.

Each of us is an original.

GALATIANS 5:26

———

Like an open book,
you watched me grow from
conception to birth;
all the stages of my life were
spread out before you.

PSALM 139:16

———

We don't reduce
Christ to what we are;
he raises us to what he is.

I CORINTHIANS 10:18

I'll call nobodies

and make them somebodies;

I'll call the unloved

and make them beloved.

ROMANS 9:25

Talking About...

Personal
Priorities

God is the living center of everything.

We plan
the way we want to live,
but only God
makes us able
to live it.

PROVERBS 16:9

- I stretch myself out. I sleep.
  Then I'm up again—rested,
  tall and steady.

  PSALM 3:5

- Go to work in the morning
  and stick to it until evening without
  watching the clock.

  ECCLESIASTES 11:6

- Keep your eye on what you're doing;
  ...do a thorough job as God's servant.

  2 TIMOTHY 4:5

- Put GOD in charge of your work,
  then what you've planned
  will take place.

  PROVERBS 16:3

Obedience is not
a stodgy plodding
in the ruts of religion,
it is a hopeful race toward
God's promises.

Work six days
and do everything
you need to do.
But the seventh day is a
Sabbath to God, your God.

EXODUS 20:8

―――――――

I inherited your book on living;
it's mine forever—
what a gift!

PSALM 119:111

―――――――

You're my place of quiet retreat;
I wait for your Word to renew me.

PSALM 119:114

Talking About...

Friends

*A person all
wrapped up in himself makes
a very small package.*

Love others
as you love yourself.
That's an act of true freedom.

GALATIANS 5:14

———

Give away your life;
you'll find life given back,...
with bonus and blessing.

LUKE 6:38

Friendship
takes what's common
in human experience and
turns it into
something holy.

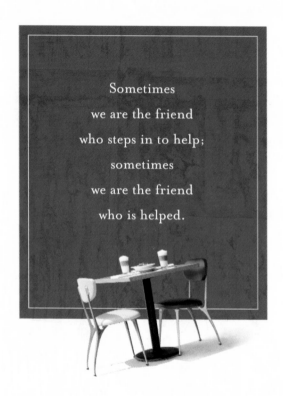

Sometimes
we are the friend
who steps in to help;
sometimes
we are the friend
who is helped.

If someone falls into sin,
forgivingly restore him. . . .
You might be needing forgiveness
before the day's out.

GALATIANS 6:1

If we love one another,
God, God swells deeply within us,
and his love becomes complete in us—
perfect love!

I JOHN 4:12

Love never gives up.
Love cares more for others than for self.

I CORINTHIANS 13:4

- Regardless of what else you put on,
  wear love.
  It's your basic, all-purpose garment.
  Never be without it.

  COLOSSIANS 3:14

- Be gracious in your speech.
  The goal is to bring out the best
  in others in a conversation,
  not put them down, not cut them out.

  COLOSSIANS 4:6

- Be good friends who love deeply;
  practice playing second fiddle.

  ROMANS 12:10

- Friends love through all kinds
  of weather.

  PROVERBS 17:17

Other people
are awesome creatures
to be respected
and befriended,
especially the ones
that I cannot get
anything out of.

Talking About...

A Money Makeover

*Worshiping God is
more central than impressing
our neighbors.*

Fulfill your obligations as a citizen.
Pay your taxes, pay your bills,
respect your leaders.

ROMANS 13:7

Don't run up debts,
except for the huge debt of love you
owe each other.

ROMANS 13:8

Don't be obsessed
with getting more material things.
Be relaxed with what you have.

HEBREWS 13:5

Reaching out
is an act of wholeness,
not only for others
but for us.

If we lose touch
with our values,
we are at the mercy
of every seduction,
every inducement,
every claim on our money,
our energy, our time.

Don't fool yourself.
Don't think that you can be wise merely by
being up-to-date with the times. . . .
What the world calls smart,
God calls stupid.

I CORINTHIANS 3:18–19

———————

Lust for money
brings trouble and nothing
but trouble.

I TIMOTHY 6:10

- Prosperity is as short-lived
  as a wildflower,
  so don't ever count on it.

JAMES 1:10

- Honor God with everything you own;
  give him the first and the best.

PROVERBS 3:9

- It's only human
  to want to make a buck,
  but it's better to be poor than a liar.

PROVERBS 19:22

- Live generously
  and graciously toward others,
  the way God lives toward you.

MATTHEW 5:48

God is generous
and never runs out
of blessings.
God delights in giving—
it's what he does best.

Talking About...

The
Lifestyle
Thing

A servant Christian is the
freest person on earth.

Nothing
counts more in the way
we live than
what we believe
about God.

Are You Talking to Me God?

- Take on an entirely new way of life—
  a God-fashioned life.

EPHESIANS 4:24

- Your life is a journey you must travel
  with a deep consciousness of God.

I PETER 1:17

- Live well, live wisely, live humbly.
  It's the way you live, not the way you talk,
  that counts.

JAMES 3:13

- Live creatively, friends.

GALATIANS 6:1

We live in a culture
where image is everything
and substance nothing. . . .
But an image without substance
is a lie.

Don't love the world's ways.
Don't love the world's goods.
Love of the world squeezes out love
for the Father.

1 JOHN 2:15

———————

A life devoted to things is a dead life,
a stump; a God-shaped life
is a flourishing tree.

PROVERBS 11:28

———————

An undisciplined,
self-willed life is puny; an obedient,
God-willed life is spacious.

PROVERBS 15:32

Talking About...

Prayer

*Prayer is the
most practical thing
anyone can do.*

Any place
is the right place to begin
to pray.
But we must not be
afraid of ending up some place
quite different from
where we start.

Ask and you'll get;
Seek and you'll find;
Knock and the door will open.

LUKE 11:9

Pile your troubles
on God's shoulders—
he'll carry your load,
he'll help you out.

PSALM 55:22

- If you don't know what you're doing,
  pray to the Father.
  He loves to help.

JAMES 1:5

- I pray to God—my life a prayer—
  and wait for what he'll say and do.

PSALM 130:5

- Thank God!
  Pray to him by name!
  Tell everyone you meet what
  he has done!

PSALM 105:1

Authentic prayer begins
when we stub our toes on a rock,
get drenched in a rainstorm,
get slapped in the face
by an enemy.

The moment I called out, you stepped in;
you made my life large with strength.

PSALM 138:3

Prayer
takes place in every
detail of life.

Are You Talking to Me God?

Pray every way you know how,
for everyone you know.

I TIMOTHY 2:1

Don't quit in hard times;
pray all the harder.

ROMANS 12:12

God's there,
listening for all who pray,
for all who pray
and mean it.

PSALM 145:18

Talking About...

Potential and
Possibilities

*Each day opens out
into a more.*

- Look up,
  and be alert to what is going on
  around Christ—
  that's where the action is.
  See things from his perspective.

  COLOSSIANS 3:2

- It's in Christ that we find out
  who we are and what we are living for.

  EPHESIANS 1:11

- God can do anything, you know—
  far more than you could ever imagine
  or guess or request in your
  wildest dreams!

  EPHESIANS 3:20

Who we are
and will be is compounded
with who God is and
what he does.

Everyone's childhood
serves up the raw material
that is shaped by grace into the
life of mature faith.

Before I shaped you in the womb,
I knew all about you.
Before you saw the light of day,
I had holy plans for you.

JEREMIAH 1:5

No one
can substitute for me.
No one can replace me.
Before I was good for anything,
God decided
that I was good for what
he was doing.

No one's ever. . .
imagined anything quite like it—
what God has arranged for those
who love him.

I CORINTHIANS 2:9

———————

Just look at it—
we're called children of God!
That's who we really are. . . .
And that's only the beginning.

I JOHN 3:1–2

Go out into the world
uncorrupted, a breath of fresh air
in this squalid and polluted society.
Provide people
with a glimpse of good
living and of the living God.

PHILIPPIANS 2:15

Talking About...

Advice and
Answers

God's ways are dependable,
his promises sure.

Christian discipleship
is making a map of
the faithfulness of God,
not charting
the rise and fall of
our enthusiasms.

- If you quit listening, dear child,
  and strike off on your own,
  you'll soon be out of your depth.

PROVERBS 19:27

- Hold tight to good advice;
  don't relax your grip.
  Guard it well.

PROVERBS 4:13

- Listen for GOD's voice
  in everything you do,
  everywhere you go;
  he's the one who will keep you
  on track.

PROVERBS 3:6

The gullible
believe anything they're told;
the prudent sift and weigh
every word.

PROVERBS 14:15

———————

Trust God
from the bottom of your heart;
don't try to figure out
everything on your own.

PROVERBS 3:5

———————

Take good counsel
and accept correction—
that's the way to live wisely and well.

PROVERBS 19:20

Life is an
entirety into which we grow,
not a fragment
that we snatch on the run.

Talking About...

Mistakes
and Messing Up

*We sing our songs
of victory in a world
where things get messy.*

Only when I recognize
and confess my sin
am I in a position to
recognize and respond
to the God who saves me
from my sin.

- He got us out of the mess we're in
  and restored us to where
  he always wanted us to be.
  And he did it by means of Jesus Christ.

  ROMANS 3:25

- The sacrificed blood of Jesus,
  God's Son,
  purges all our sin.

  1 JOHN 1:7

- If we claim that we're free of sin,
  we're only fooling ourselves. . . .
  On the other hand, if we admit our sins—
  make a clean breast of them—
  . . . he'll forgive our sins and purge us
  of all wrongdoing.

  1 JOHN 1:8–9

The subtlety of sin
is that it doesn't feel like sin
when we're doing it;
it feels godlike.

Scrub away my guilt,
soak out my sins in your laundry.

PSALM 51:2

———————

God's business is putting things right;
he loves getting the lines straight,
setting us straight.

PSALM 11:7

———————

He forgives your sins—every one.

PSALM 103:3

We wander
like lost sheep,
true; but God is a
faithful shepherd who pursues
us relentlessly.

Why do we easily imagine
God tenderly watching over
a falling sparrow
but boggle at believing that he
is present in the hugger-mugger
of smoke-filled rooms?

Every detail in our lives of love for God
is worked into something good.

ROMANS 8:28

Talking About...

God
in Life

God is the living center of life.

Put your hope in God and
know real blessing!

PSALM 146:5

God-friendship is for
God-worshippers.

PSALM 25:14

God's name
is a place of protection—
good people can
run there and be safe.

PROVERBS 18:10

If we separate
any part of our lives
from God,
we are left holding
an empty bag.

The basic conviction
of a Christian is that God
intends good for us
and that he will get
his way in us.

- Trust GOD from the bottom
  of your heart;
  don't try to figure out everything
  on your own.

PROVERBS 3:5

- Absolutely nothing
  can get between us
  and God's love.

ROMANS 8:39

- GOD sticks by all who love him.

PSALM 145:20

Mostly what God does
is love you.
Keep company with him and
learn a life of love.

EPHESIANS 5:1

Your love, GOD,
fills the earth!
Train me to live
by your counsel.

PSALM 119:64

God provides
for us and loves and
blesses and
saves us.